D1586714

Have you ever taken a snapshot like this one? Just as the button was pressed a bus shot past in front of the camera. Other things were also moving and they look blurred. To most people this is very annoying and they think that the picture is spoiled. What do you think?

Well, a blurred picture may not be completely spoiled. It really depends on what you want it to show. Often a photograph which shows things or people in motion, even if they are blurred, has a lot more life than a perfectly sharp photograph. It seems to have caught an important part of life: movement. The picture on this page is interesting because it shows movement. The blurring has not spoiled the picture; it has added something to it.

Here are two pictures of pigeons. The first is very clear and sharp. The second is largely blurred because the pigeons were moving. But this does not mean that the picture is less good. The movement of the pigeons has become a part of the picture. If you want a picture which shows all the details the first is better. What are the advantages and the disadvantages of the second? Here are some more objects which were photographed while they were moving. They show us something rather important about these objects: we can see how they moved. In the first picture the hand may be simply holding the pages of the book or it

may be flicking the pages; we cannot be sure. But in the second picture there is no doubt; we can see the pages falling. The second picture tells us more about the action of the hand and the book. Likewise from looking at the other two pictures on this page we understand how the musician's hands move and how the tin lid spins on the table top.

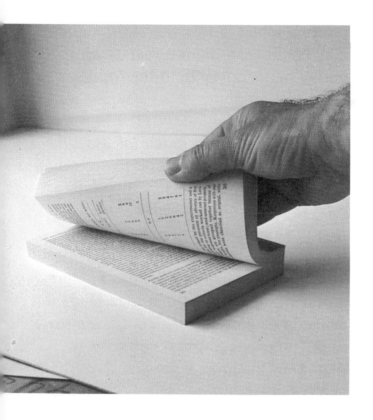

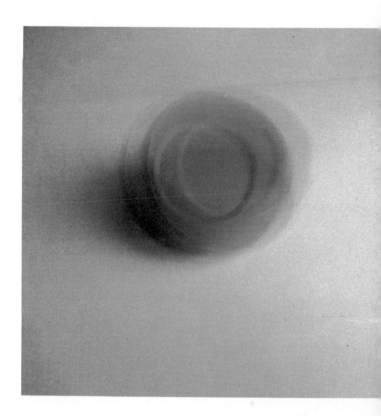

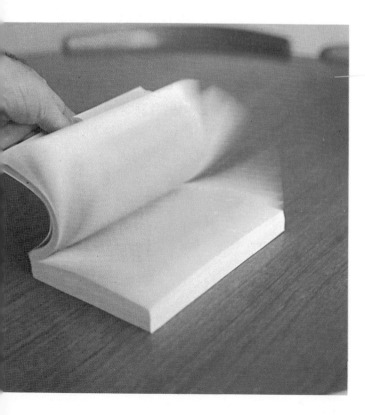

The cardboard shapes are hung from thin threads. The slightest current of air makes them move about and spin. The three pictures were taken while they were moving. What do they show? The faster and farther a thing moves the more blurred it will become when it is photographed in this way. In the end it may become so blurred that it can hardly be recognised. In the top left-hand picture opposite we can see a person moving about, but the movement must have been too much for the camera so that it is difficult to see what is going on. The dancer in the picture next to it has moved so far and so fast that we can barely tell that we are looking at a human figure.

There is another way of photographing a moving object, and that is to take several fast pictures instead of one slow one. The photographer who took the picture of the athlete did just that. We can see the different stages of the flight of the athlete's body through the air, changing its shape as it moves across the picture. Had the photographer taken a slower picture the details would have appeared blurred but he had a special camera which could take repeated fast shots and so he could show us several positions of the moving body.

The artist who painted the picture of a dog being taken for a walk also painted several positions of each moving thing in the picture: the dog's feet, nose, and tail, the woman's feet, the chain; even the glints in the chain can be seen to be moving along. If this picture looks different from so many other pictures that you may have seen it is because the artist tried to tell us something about the way in which the things in the picture move. The artist must have thought that movement is a very important part of life. A picture which only shows what things look like when they are standing still is not always complete. It may need to show how they move. Do you think this artist succeeded in making us understand something about movement?

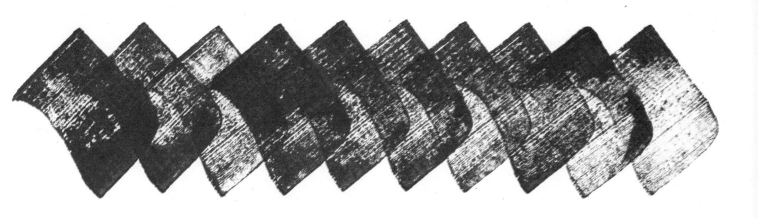

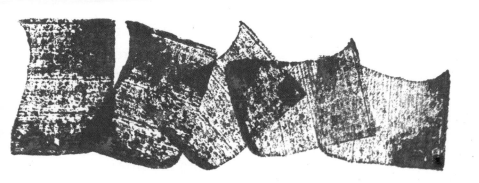

We can make pictures of moving shapes in quite a simple way. Not only human shapes or shapes in which we can recognise something we have seen before but shapes in which we cannot recognise anything. We have met many such shapes in the first two books. We call them *abstract* shapes. Here is an abstract shape moving forward. You can see that it is really a piece of wood which has been inked and printed several times. You could do the same with a potato cut or lino cut. Each print marks the position of the shape in its movement. It is similar to the different positions of the athlete flying through the air.

The second picture shows a shape moving forward and falling at the same time: two movements in one.

Another shape is doing a complete turn in its path.

In the bottom picture on page 5 we saw the movements of a man jumping. Not only is he moving forward, but we can see his limbs and trunk moving as well. The overall shape of his body is changing as it moves along.
We can do the same with an abstract shape. Above a shape is moving forward and changing at the same time.

The two pictures below also show a moving shape which changes as it moves: a tablecloth drying on the line. The wind blows it about. The first picture shows how we normally see it in photographs and posters. The second picture shows several positions of the tablecloth as it is being blown about by the breeze. When we look at this picture we realise that the first picture shows only one of the many positions of the fluttering tablecloth.

Let us now go back to printing shapes which move. In the top picture opposite a shape similar to the shape on page 7 has been printed many times. Each print indicates a position of the same shape as it moved. But here the spaces between the prints are all different. It looks as though the shape had slowed

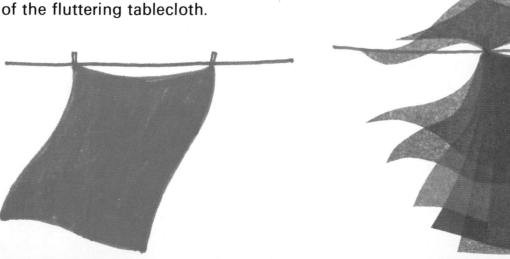

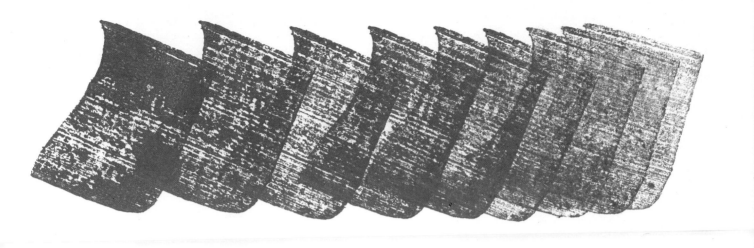

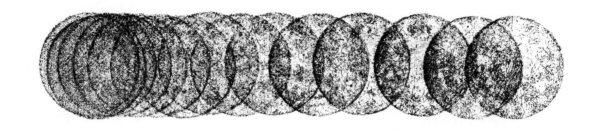

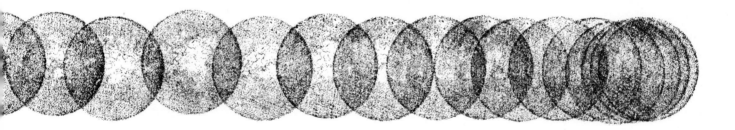

down. How would you describe the movement of the round disc in the second picture on this page? The very long picture of the moving disc shows the disc moving off slowly at first, gathering speed and slowing down again. When it moved slowly the prints are closer together; when it moved faster the prints are farther apart. In this way we can make pictures not only of movement but also of speed. We can show different speeds of the same movement. We can do this even when the path of the moving shape is curved as in the last picture

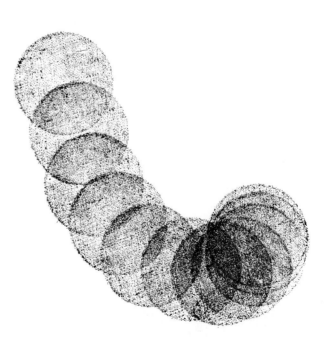

The photograph of the man swinging an Indian club was taken with a special camera. It shows the club in many positions on its path. If you look closely you will see that the spaces are not all the same. Can you tell from this picture where the club was travelling fastest, where slowest?

We have seen how we may draw or print a shape which is moving along a straight or curved path and changing speed. But sometimes it may move in yet another way at the same time. The shape in this picture wobbles as it moves and changes speed. We can tell from looking at the picture.

In the top picture a bottle is floating on the water, drifting slowly. Can you tell where the bottle was travelling slowly or where a small current was speeding it up? What else can you tell from the picture?

In the composition below a number of shapes can be seen moving in straight and curved paths, changing speed and form, wobbling.

These two pictures show street scenes. They are rather similar but there is one very important difference. Can you tell what it is? As in most busy streets some of the things are moving while others are still. In which picture can you see most clearly which things are moving and which things are still? Can you tell in which direction they are moving?

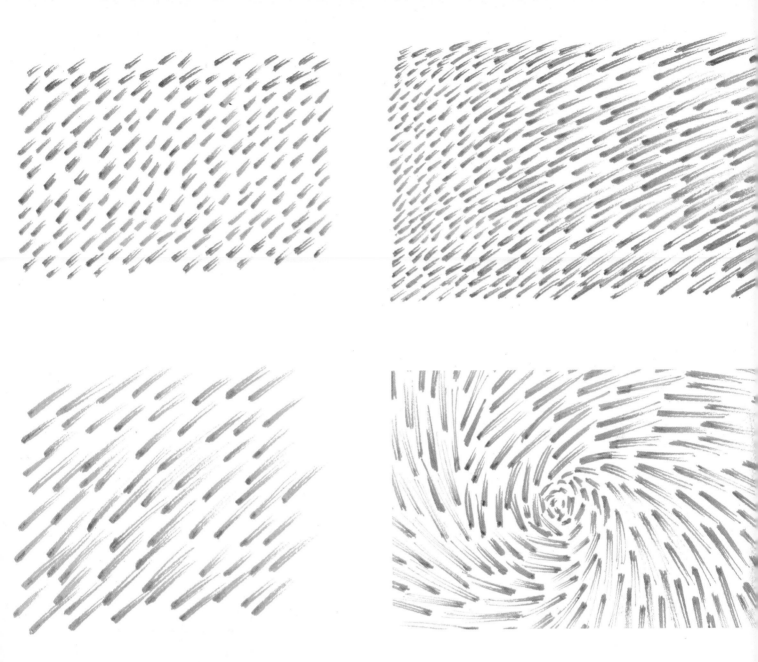

In the second street picture you will notice that some of the moving things are more blurred than others.
The cars are more blurred than the people. The reason is that during the time it took to take the picture the cars travelled farther than the pedestrians. You may understand this better if you look at the drawing. So we can tell two important things from this photograph. We can see which things were moving and which were still. We can also see which were fast and which were slow.

The four drawings on this page show raindrops falling through the air. In the first picture the raindrops are not falling straight down because a slight wind is blowing them sideways.
In the next picture the wind is much stronger. We can see that each drop is being blown more to one side and travelling farther. In the third drawing the raindrops are travelling at different speeds. What do you think is the cause? What do you think is happening in the fourth drawing?

We have considered many different kinds of movement but there is still one kind which we have not yet spoken of and which is at least as important as all others. Imagine you look at a leaf of a plant during the growing season and you draw it in its proper size.

A few days later you may find it has grown in size and slightly changed its shape. You draw it again.

Yet a few days later you look at it once more and draw it. Now it looks like this.

Finally you draw it yet again in its fully grown state.

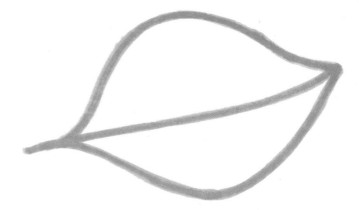

If you had done these drawings on thin paper and put one on top of the other so that you can see them all together they might look like this.

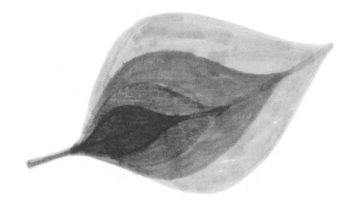

You will see at once that this is rather like the pictures on page 7 but instead of moving along the leaf has grown and moved outwards. It has also taken much longer to do it. That is why growth is difficult to see, but as this drawing shows, growth is a kind of movement.

Of course growth may take other forms as well, for instance like this

or like this

Can you find the different stages of growth in these drawings? Can you think of other kinds of growth and how to draw them?

In Learning to See we sometimes look at shapes which we can recognise such as flowers, trees, houses and cars, and sometimes at abstract shapes, that is to say shapes in which we cannot recognise anything. You will remember we made patterns from flowers and also from abstract shapes. In a pattern or composition abstract shapes mean just as much as recognisable shapes.
Let us now take some abstract shapes and make them grow, as though they were flowers or trees or animals. Here are some.

Follow their growth from the centre outwards and you will notice that they grow in different ways. Also some grow more on one side than on the other.

In the following drawings the stages
of growth are not as clear as in the
last drawings. We might compare them
to the pictures on pages 2 and 3. But
we understand from them how the
movement of growth has taken place.

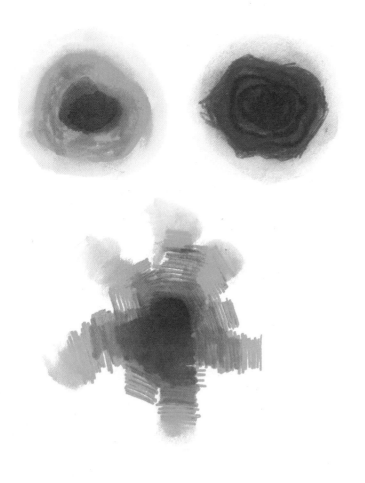

On the right is a composition of flat
shapes. Some are still, they do not
move nor grow. Can you tell which
they are? Other shapes are growing.
Some of them have grown towards
each other and into each other. Two
of them are overlapping. They all grow
in different ways and at different
speeds. Can you tell the difference?

You must already have seen pictures of fireworks like the one here. What makes the lines in such a picture? The exploding firework does not shoot out lines into the sky but many little lit-up dots. The lines you see in this photograph are the paths of tiny fiery dots. Each line shows the movement of one dot.

The night picture above also shows the paths of moving dots. Each dot is the light of a car and as the cars moved along the camera captured their movements in a way which the eye cannot. Why not?

It is possible to make a drawing in this way. The picture at the top of page 19 was made by moving a torch about in a dark room. If a drawing made with a pencil is called a pencil drawing, then this should be called a light drawing. The two smaller pictures on the right were made in a similar way. A torch was fastened to the end of a piece of string. to make a pendulum. It was photographed from below as it swung freely. Each picture shows a different

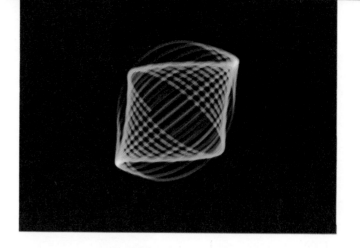

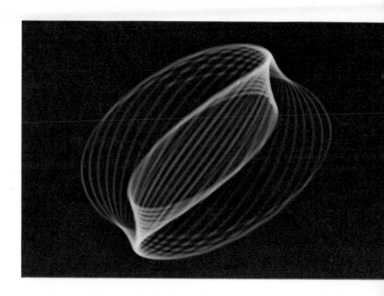

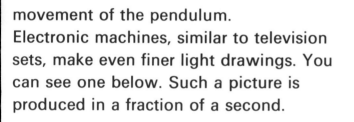

movement of the pendulum.
Electronic machines, similar to television
sets, make even finer light drawings. You
can see one below. Such a picture is
produced in a fraction of a second.

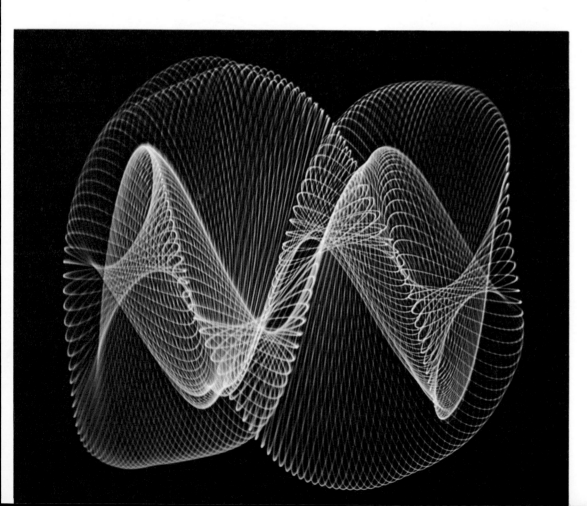

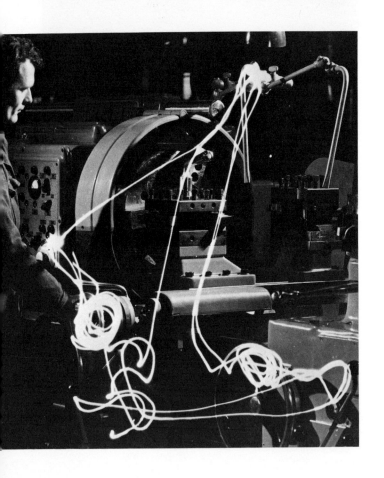

Photographs of this kind are very useful for many purposes. This picture shows a worker at a machine. A light has been fixed to his right hand. As his hand moved while he was operating the machine the camera photographed the moving light. The photograph shows the movement of his hand very clearly. Designers study photographs like this when they design new machines. In what way do you think such photographs can help them?

The drawing below was made with a machine which moves rather like a pendulum. A felt-tip pen was fixed to it and the moving pen produced the drawing. It shows the path of the tip of the pen just as the pictures on page 19 show the path of a light.

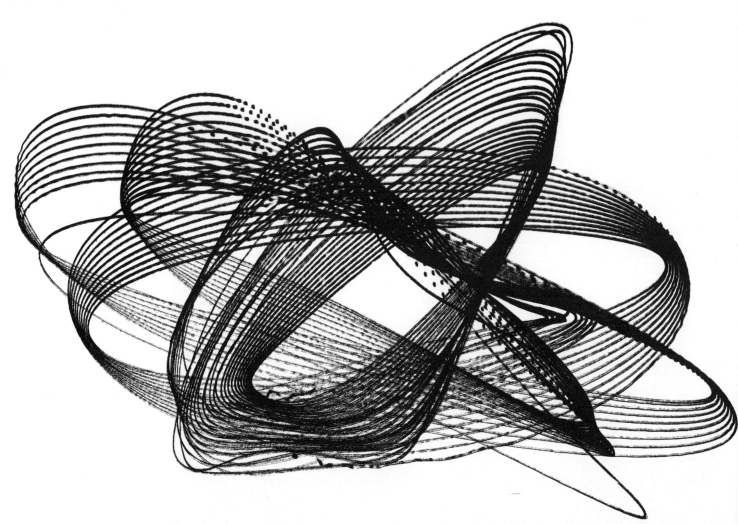

Suppose that the conductor of an orchestra has been watched. The line describes the movement of his right hand. But if you were to watch another conductor – perhaps conducting the same piece of music – you might find that his hand moves in a slightly different way, as in the second drawing. Yet another conductor would probably move even more differently, as in the third drawing. You will notice that the main movements are very similar but they still vary from each other. Each one has been carried out in a slightly different way. Why do you think this is?

We can think of all lines, not only those made by lights, as paths of moving dots or points. Each of the lines you see here shows the movement of a point. Each line tells us something about the movement. Can you imitate these movements, one by one, in the air with the tip of your finger? Could you have described these movements in any other way?

We do not have to fix a light to a person's hand to find out how it is moving. We can watch his hand very carefully and then draw a line which describes the movement. Here is such a drawing.

We can see not only the broad movements in the drawings on page 21, but by comparing the three pictures we may also see the particular way in which each movement was carried out. Each one of the conductors had his own way of conducting and moving his hand through the air.

Human beings are on the whole very similar but they are also different from each other. You can recognise your friends even in a crowd because they are all different. You might recognise their voices even if you could not see them. You might recognise them even if they are disguised or in fancy dress. Each person has a different *character*. The lines describe the movements of different conductors. We can say the lines have different characters.

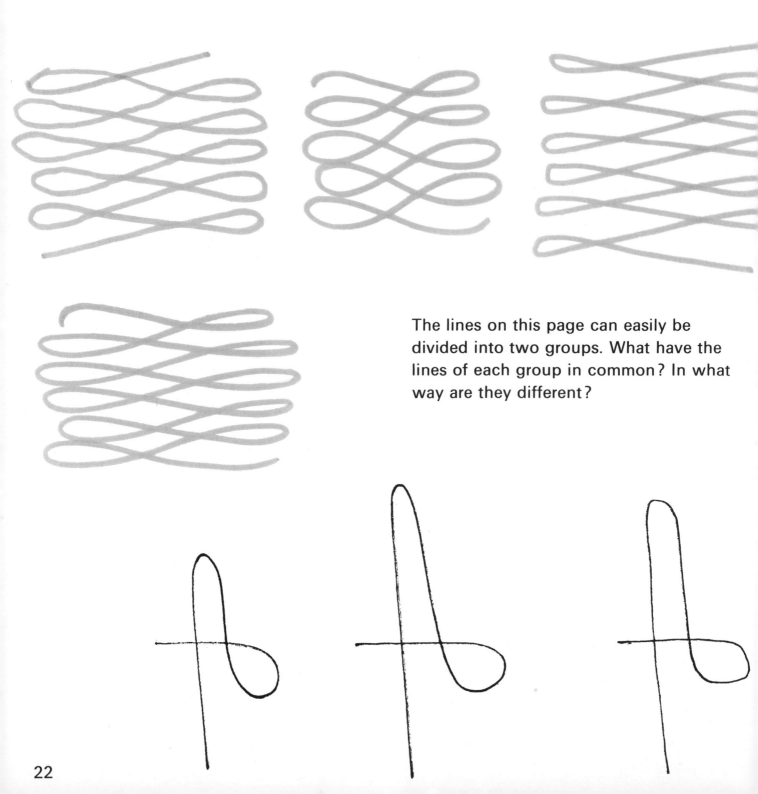

The lines on this page can easily be divided into two groups. What have the lines of each group in common? In what way are they different?

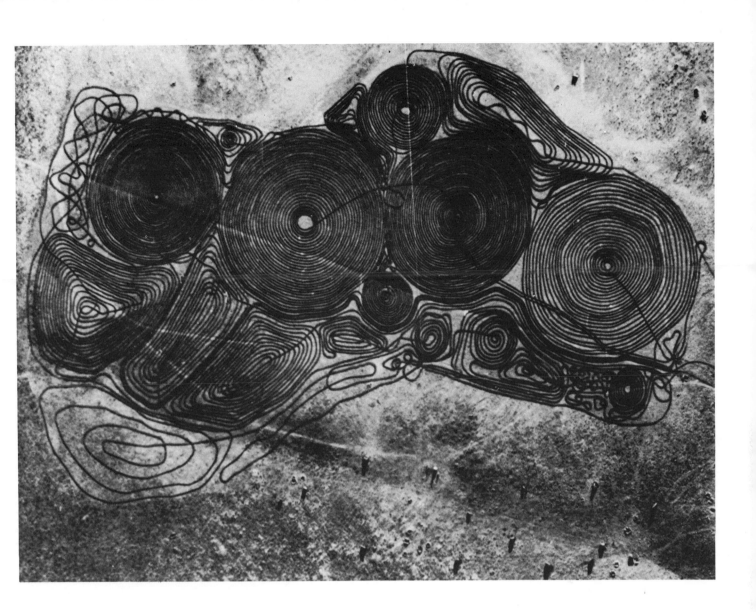

This picture was taken during the war by RAF planes in the Middle East. The Germans were retreating, and before abandoning an airfield they ploughed it up so that the RAF could not use it. They used several ploughs and each one covered part of the ground in the form of a spiral. This makes a fascinating pattern when seen from the air. We must remember that it was made by a number of dots (ploughs) moving about rather like the lights on page 19. Each one is the path of a moving dot or point. The lines of icing on a cake are also the path of a moving point.

In the first book we looked at related shapes and the patterns and compositions we can make from them. Movements and the lines which describe them may also be related and made into a pattern or a composition. In this picture several lines are combined in one pattern. Like the related shapes in Book 1 these lines seem to have something in common and to belong together. They all start with a more or less straight path and then curl away, some to the left some to the right, in whirls of different sizes and characters. Together they fall into a large pattern of movements.

These lines are also related to each other. Although they are all different there is always some part of a line which follows another. They all have something in common.

The composition on the left consists of lines of different thicknesses. How are they related?

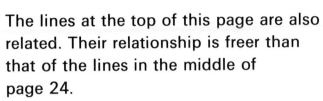

The lines at the top of this page are also related. Their relationship is freer than that of the lines in the middle of page 24.

The drawing on the right consists of two sets of related lines coming from opposite directions like two jets of smoke, one enveloping the other. The sets of lines are related to each other. We can see this relationship more clearly if we draw them in different colours.

The picture at the bottom was drawn by the machine which did the drawing on page 20. The lines are drawn in different colours so that their free relationship is shown.

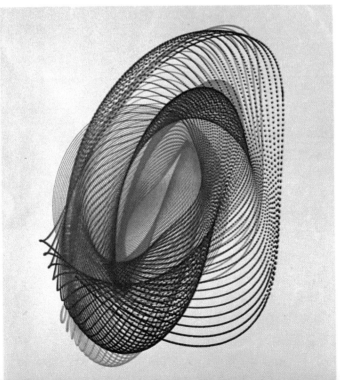

The paths of cars and lorries in traffic are related to each other. In this picture which is rather like a map the large red shapes are houses, the blue one is a pond, the green one a park. The traffic flows between them. Each line in this picture is the path of a car, lorry or motorcycle. No two paths are exactly the same but together they form a harmonious pattern.

The pattern of lines made by the traffic fits into the pattern made by the houses, pond and lake. They are related. This is a relationship of moving things and still things, of lines and shapes. Do you think the lines of the London Underground are related to each other?

We can often find such relationships. Imagine that a dog enters an old ruined building. He will run round about inside it, nose to the ground, perhaps trying to pick up a scent. He will also explore the outside of the house. Having found nothing to interest him he will run away. The dog's movements are shown in this picture. They are related to the ruins which are also shown. If we look at this picture as a composition we can see that lines and shapes are related. In the second picture we do not see an event such as the one in the last picture but abstract shapes and moving lines. They are related. Could one call this a composition?

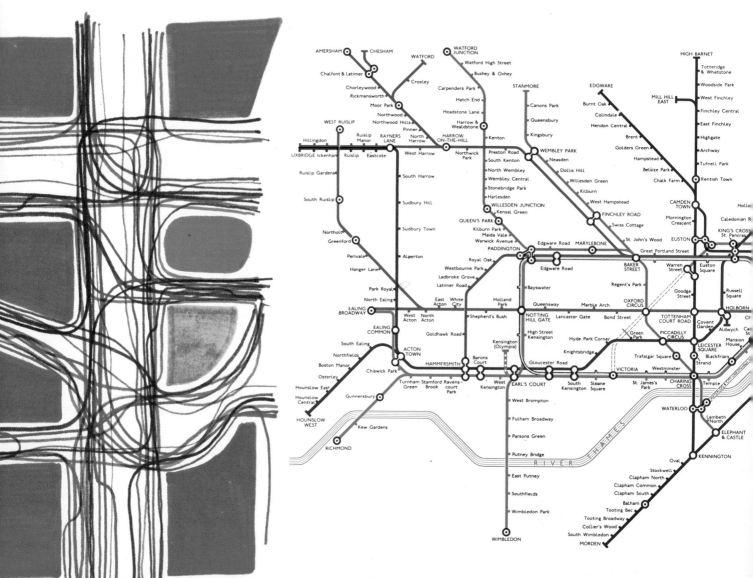

Here are some more compositions of abstract shapes and lines of movement. There is nothing here that you might recognise. Try and remember the compositions of abstract shapes in Book 1. Do you think it is an advantage to have lines and movements as well as shapes which are still? Can you think when such compositions might be useful?

Chapter

3

We have learned to draw and make pictures of moving things and of movement itself. Let us now see how useful such drawings may be. In the drawing on the right you see how the combined movements of football players lead to a goal being scored. One side is shown in green, the other in red, the path of the ball in blue. Can you follow the whole event starting in the bottom left-hand corner? How many movements can you see altogether? Are they related to each other?

The picture below, left, shows a story from the Old Testament, the story of Jael and Sisera.

Can you tell what is happening?

The road sign also consists of lines which show movement.

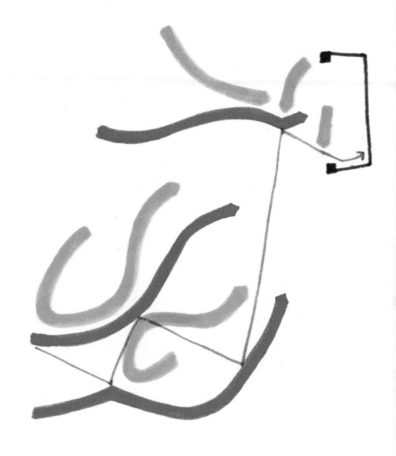

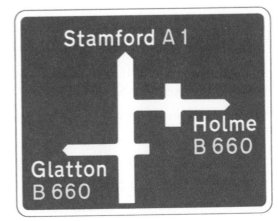

This composition shows several movements. A flower and several grasses are swaying to and fro in the wind. Different kinds of insects are buzzing about, one of them actually enters the flower and leaves again. A white cloud drifts by. What else can you tell from this picture?

We have seen that movement — or several movements — may be related to shapes. The picture on the next page is similar to the one on page 26 of the moving cars amongst houses. It shows a school and other buildings. The lines describe the paths of children going to school. We can see that some children are crossing the road together, others are walking along the pavement together, one child is actually going back in order to join a friend and so on.

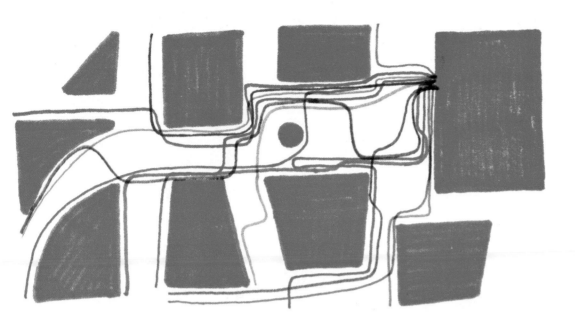

But somehow the picture is still not quite complete. For, as you know, some children walk slowly, others run, some walk quickly and without showing these differences in speed we cannot say that the picture is a good description of the scene.

So we must try and invent a way of showing speed as well as movement. We do not need to show the exact speed but it is important to know which movement is faster and which slower.

Let us think again of the icing on the cake. If you decorate a cake with icing which is not too stiff but quite free-flowing you will soon learn that the more quickly you move the icing pump the thinner the line gets. If you move the pump more slowly the cream which comes out of the tip piles up and makes the line thicker. You may observe something very much like this if you draw with a free-flowing pen on newsprint, tissue paper, or blotting paper. The quickly-drawn lines are the thinnest; as soon as your pen slows down the line gets thicker. If you look

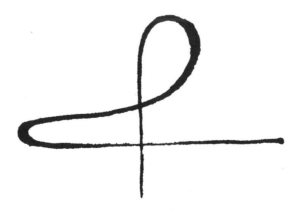

at the photograph of the machine
worker's hand movements you will
notice that the long straight movements
which are normally done quickly are
also the thinnest, the curved parts of
the path which are slower are thicker.
Here is a detail from the picture on
page 20.

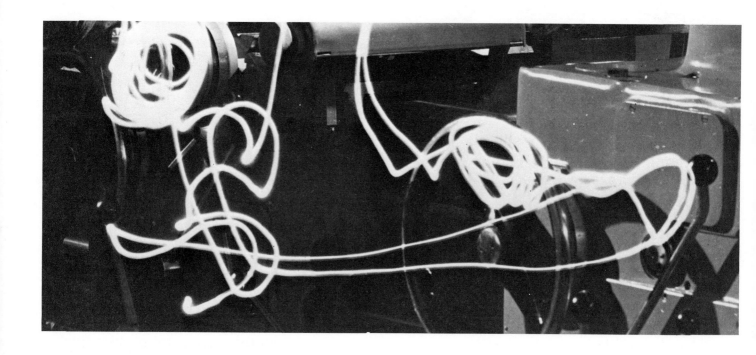

So let us try and show differences of
speed by varying the thickness of the
line: thinner for faster movement,
thicker for slower movement. These
two drawings show the path of a
racing car going round a racing circuit.
The first drawing shows only the path
of the moving car, but in the second
we see how the driver slows down for
the bends (thick line) and speeds along
the straight parts of the track (thin
line). The line is thickest in the
tightest bends. In this way we can
show the changing speed of the car.
We can also combine two or more
movements which have different
speeds.

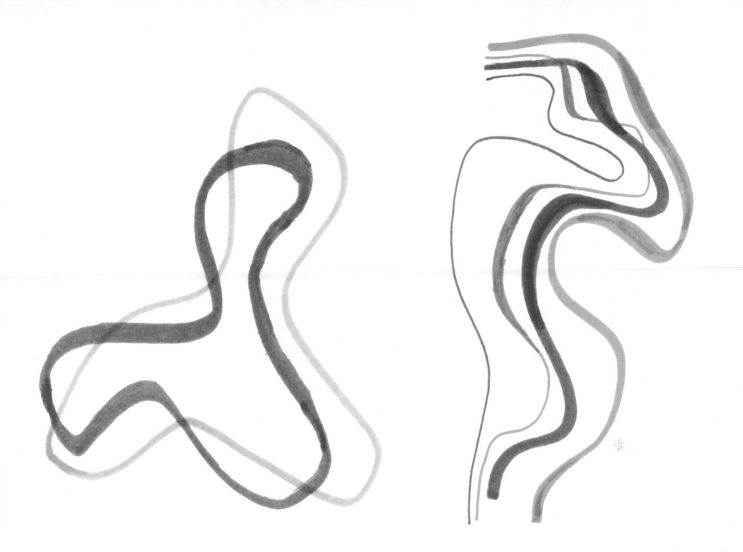

The two closed lines describe two movements which seem to be chasing each other. But while one of them speeds up and slows down as it goes round the other maintains the same speed all the time.

Lines which are not closed but go from one point to another may also be related as in the drawing above. Three of the lines move more or less together, but at varying speeds; the fourth crosses the centre line in three places. The five lines which run from one side of the page to the other show movements which cross and recross at ever-changing speeds.

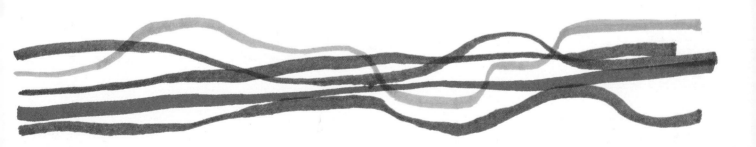

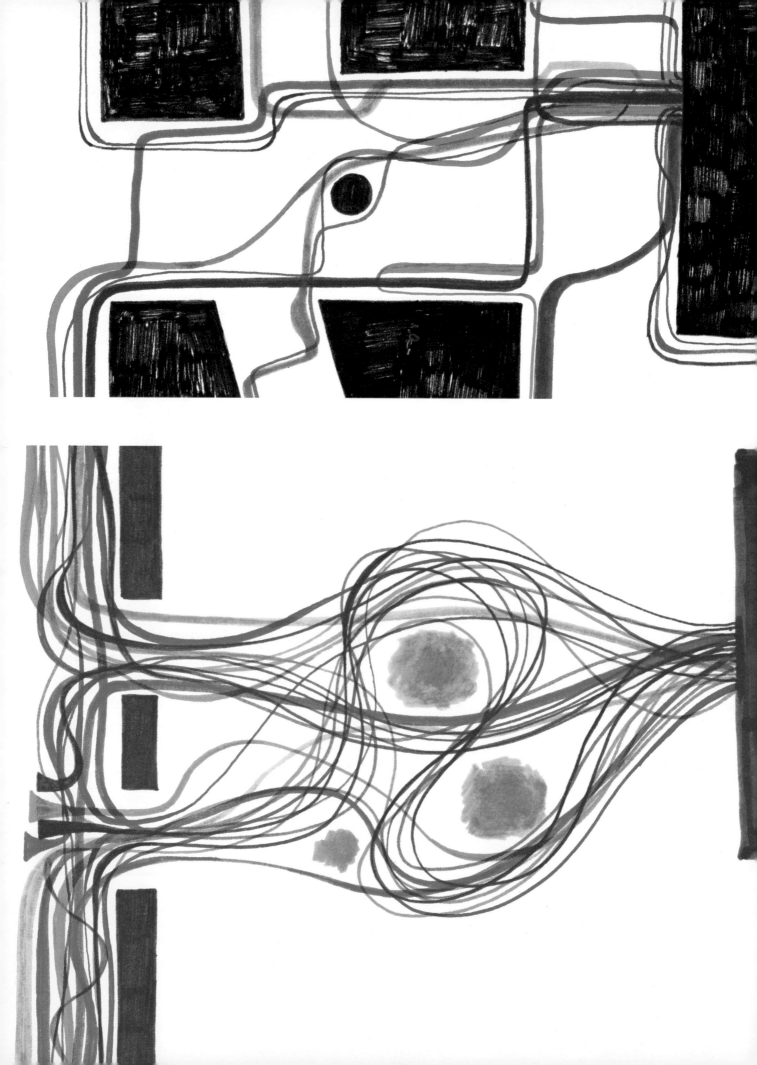

Now we may return to the problem with which we started, the children going to school. On the left is a similar composition but there are fewer lines than in the picture on page 31 so that the different speeds may be clearly seen. Let us now do a picture of children leaving school. The second picture shows the school and its wall with two gates. There are three trees and shrubs which the children must avoid on their way out. The children are walking and running in different paths and at different speeds. They do not run onto the road; they slow down and turn onto the pavement.

This composition shows a man, a child and a dog walking through a park. Can you tell which line is the path of the man, which of the child and which is the path of the dog? What else can you see in the picture?

Movements are not always large and sweeping, sometimes they are small and wiggly like the one in this drawing. The line covers a whole area with similar curves. Do you think we could call it a pattern? We could contrast such a tight movement with a sweeping movement as in the second picture. We could also contrast different movements in the way shown below.

In the picture above three pattern-like movements overlap. The three patterns are different from each other but the area where they overlap has something in common with all of them, rather like the overlapping areas on pages 40 and 41 of Book 1.

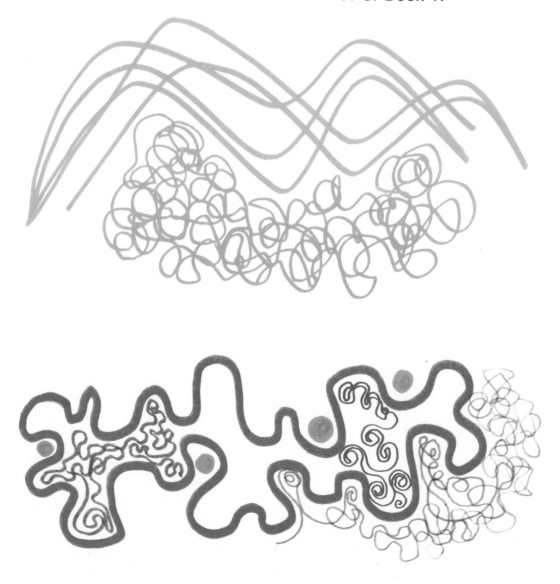

We have already seen how the character of lines and movements may be changed, but there is also another way. We can draw the lines with different things, such as pen, crayon, brush, felt-tip. Even though the lines above, right, describe the same movements they have different characters. Let us look again at the composition of movements on page 25. We can contrast the two movements even more by giving one of them a different character from the other. In what way has the composition changed?

The related lines below have different characters. Do you think the composition is better for it?

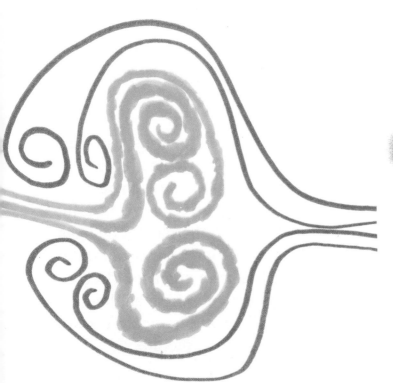

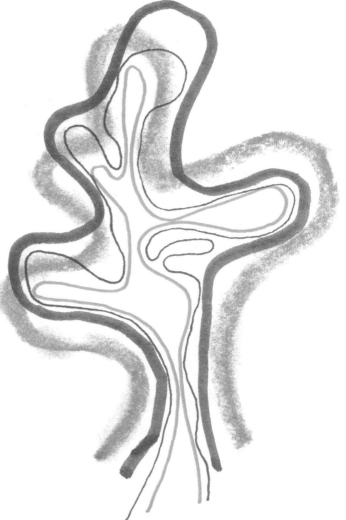

We can make lines by dripping paint from a tin onto paper instead of drawing them. We can change the character of the lines by making the hole in the tin from which it is allowed to drip larger or smaller, or the paint thicker or thinner.

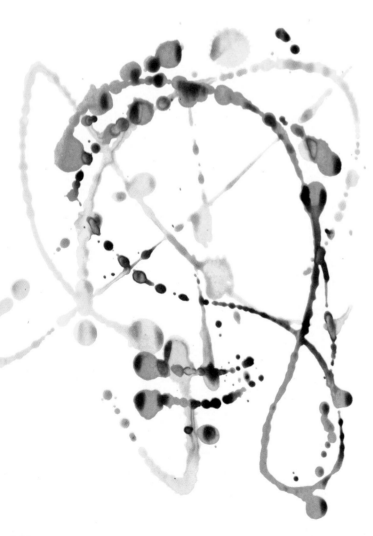

The picture above was made by allowing coloured inks to drip onto a sheet of paper. Then the paper was tilted in different directions so that the ink ran off. There are therefore in this picture two kinds of lines, each expressing a different kind of movement. Can you tell which is which?

The picture on the right was also made by dripping paint onto a surface. Remember that each line is the outcome of movement, in this case the movement of the can holding the paint. The lines are different from each other not only in colour but also in character. Because they overlap they combine all their different qualities in one richly-textured and richly-patterned picture.

We have looked at, drawn and painted many shapes and their movements in this book. It may have occurred to you that some of these may not be quite accurate. They are printed on paper and paper is usually flat, especially in a book. But not all movement is flat. For instance the floating bottle on page 11 wobbles from left to right but it is likely to have swayed also from front to back, towards you and away again. The conductor's hand may have moved forwards and backwards so that the line describing the movement should have come in front of the paper at times or gone through and behind it. We could get round this difficulty by bending the paper like this:

but this would be very inconvenient. Another way would be to use a thin piece of wire instead of a line on a flat piece of paper. We may imagine this wire to be the path of a moving point in exactly the same way as the lines on page 18, but the wire moves in space instead of on a flat piece of paper. Because it moves in space it looks quite different from different points of view, like our solid shapes in Book 2. To understand it properly we must look at it from different angles.

With a more complicated movement such as the one in the photographs on the far right it is even more important to look at it from different angles if we are to get a good idea of it.

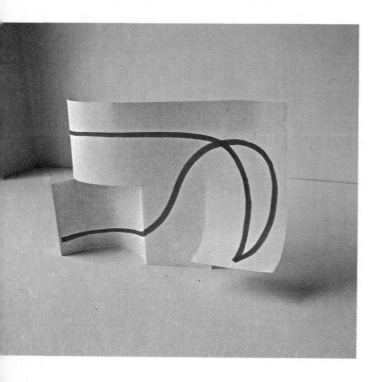

This sculpture describes a movement rather than a solid shape. You may start at any point and follow it right round.

We may combine two such movements which move freely about in space in the same way as we combined flat movements. The first picture below shows a composition. But if the same kind of wire is used throughout it may be difficult to see the different parts. It may therefore be better to paint one of them in a different colour as we did on page 25. Now we can see the contrasting characters of the two movements.

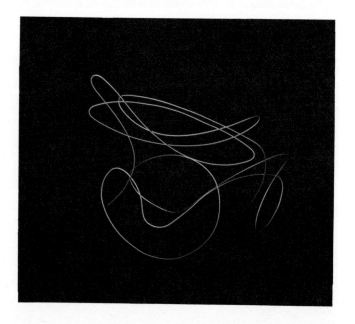

As with other compositions we can arrange the parts in different ways. The two pictures below show the same two movements arranged in another composition. Again different views will help us to understand the relationship between them.

This is a picture of the working parts of a V2 rocket used during the war. What has it in common with the pictures we have seen so far in this chapter?

Movement in space can be treated like flat movement in many ways. For instance, we may describe its changing speed. In this sculpture an artist has described a smooth curving movement which changes speed as it goes along. As in flat movement the thin line shows a fast speed, the thick line a slow speed. Imitate the movement in the air. The polished surface of the sculpture — it is made of brass — makes the movement it describes even smoother.

We may also change the quality of the line as we did with flat movements, for instance on page 38. But we must always remember that such a line will look different when viewed from different angles, as we can see from these two pictures. Again we may

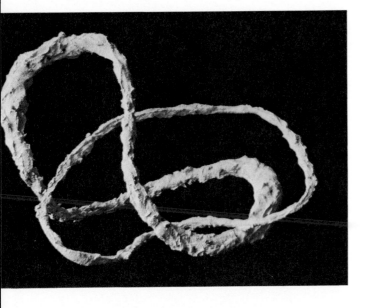

compose two or more such lines. In these compositions one line has different speeds while the other goes round at the same speed.

Where several such lines are used together, as shown below, the effect is somewhat like that of the painting on page 39, but since this is movement in space we can look at such a composition from different angles and get different impressions. Is this as richly-textured and richly-patterned as the painting?

When a point moves it produces a line. Let us now consider a short straight line in motion. When it moves as in this drawing it will make a ribbon-like flat shape. But what happens when

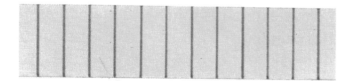

it moves through space and not over a flat surface?
We can indicate some of the positions of the moving line, similar to the shapes on page 9. This strip is the path

of the moving line. If we wish to see what happens when the line travels through space we must first of all cut it out. If we now twist or bend the strip of paper the line on it will still appear to be moving along but in a

twisting movement as it could not have done on a flat piece of paper. We can bend the strip into many different fascinating shapes, similar to those on page 4 of Book 2. The line will of course follow the paper. It is easy to imagine when looking at such a shape how the line has travelled in a twisting and turning path. The different positions of the line are at angles to each other.

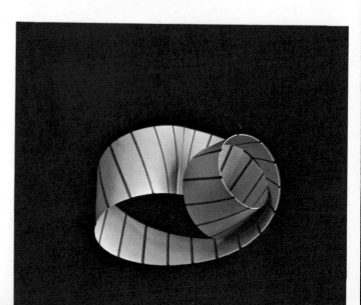

This sculpture also describes the movement of a line but the artist has left out the paper. We can see better how the line has travelled through space in a screw-wise fashion because we can see through it. The whole is suspended from a thread. It is driven by a motor to turn slowly.

It is not only in sculpture that we can see moving lines. The partly-collapsed fence in the picture above shows a similar screw-like movement. Can you think of other everyday things which show lines moving in space?

In this sculpture an artist has contrasted the movement of a line with the movement of a point. The line, sloping towards the base, moves in a stately circle. The point by contrast whirls round it in many carefree loops.

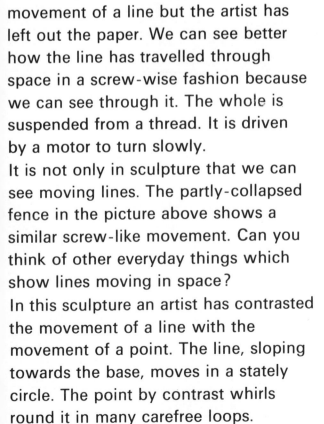

This sculpture is a large complicated shape. It has many curving surfaces and hollows. Like all great pieces of sculpture it changes shape harmoniously as we walk round it. But if we look closer we can see that the whole sculpture consists of the paths of moving lines. It is like a dance of lines whose paths have turned solid.

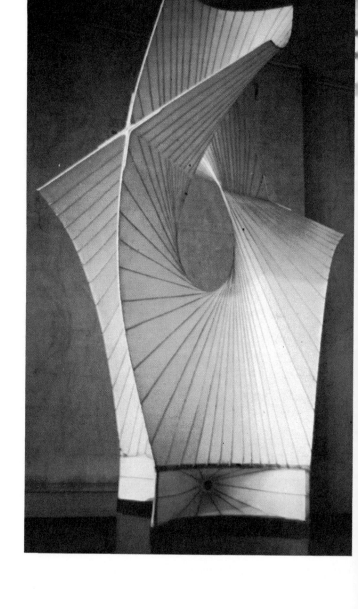

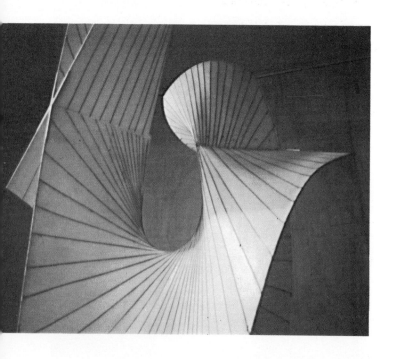